Get Well!

To

_____

From

_____

Date

_____

Get Well!

hugs
eXpreSSioNS of the Heart™

Get Well!

HOWARD BOOKS
A Division of Simon & Schuster

New York   London   Toronto   Sidney

Our purpose at Howard Books is to:
• *Increase faith* in the hearts of growing Christians
• *Inspire holiness* in the lives of believers
• *Instill hope* in the hearts of struggling people everywhere
Because He's coming again!

HOWARD
BOOKS

Published by Howard Books, a division of Simon & Schuster
1230 Avenue of the Americas, New York, NY 10020

Get Well! © 2006 by Howard Books

ISBN 13: 978-1-58229-563-3
ISBN 10:   1-58229-563-8

10 9 8 7 6 5 4 3 2 1

HOWARD is a registered trademark of Simon & Schuster, Inc.

Manufactured in China

For information regarding special discounts for bulk purchases, please contact Simon & Schuster Special Sales at 1-800-456-6798 or business@simonandschuster.com.

Contributors: Ginger Young and Janet Smith
Edited by Philis Boultinghouse
Cover design by Terry Dugan Design
Interior design by Stephanie D. Walker

Contents

Gentle Strength 1

Enthusiasm 15

Touch 27

Well Wishes 39

Endless Hope 53

Laughter 67

Love 79

Gentle Strength

Enthusiasm

Touch

Well Wishes

Endless Hope

Laughter

Love

CHAPTER 1

Gentle Strength

True strength is grown only through adversity, it seems. And when the pains of life come our way, we have a choice in how we respond. Some react to life's challenges with bitterness and resentment, while the souls of others develop a gentle strength that nothing can destroy.

Through bouts of ill health, these strong ones demonstrate nothing but a gentle strength and a stubborn confidence that the illness will not break them. They have a voracious resolve to be well that fuels their recovery and inspires everyone around them.

Hang in there! Your strength is an inspiration to us all.

WHAT LIES BEHIND US
AND WHAT LIES BEFORE US
ARE TINY MATTERS
COMPARED TO WHAT LIES WITHIN US.

Ralph Waldo Emerson

THE BEST WAY
OUT OF A DIFFICULTY
IS THROUGH IT.

Author Unknown

• The Blessing of Uncertainties •

hy is it that people always whisper in hospital halls? Angela asked herself as she sat up in her bed, adjusted the pillows behind her back, and tried to determine exactly what the pattern was on her ever-so-unattractive hospital gown. She appreciated this brief moment of solitude. A doctor would walk through the door at any moment, she knew, and her long wait would be over. She needed this quiet time to prepare herself to face the results of her tests.

Angela's friend Anna had accompanied her to the hospital this morning, and Angela was grateful. But truly, she was not afraid. She knew she would be able to find the strength to deal with whatever the doctor told her, just as she had always done whenever life had thrown challenges her way.

Anna was now in the cafeteria, trying to find a sandwich and a cup of coffee that didn't taste three days old. Angela was glad that her friend was taking care of her growling stomach and not hovering over her, constantly fidgeting and wondering out loud about the tests and their possible results. Angela knew her friend meant well, but her nervous energy was a bit tiring.

Angela reached over to open the blinds at the window and then closed her eyes as the sunshine poured in. The bright rays warmed her face and made her feel relaxed and a little drowsy. Opening her eyes slowly, she gazed up into the bright blue sky dotted with puffs of white. She watched as the clouds moved and changed shapes, dancing gracefully with the wind.

Every time Angela watched this dance across the sky, she remembered the hours of pleasure she had found as a little girl sprawled on the ground and staring into the heavens with her older sister, Eva. Imagination had been their guide as they took turns narrating the stories told by the clouds passing overhead.

It is often said that your life passes before your eyes as the day of death draws near. Though her mind was filled with recollections of times past, Angela knew that today was not that day. She had simply learned to store away memories in her own mental picture album and retrieve them at the moment she needed them. These pictures of meaningful people and places were always available; they could never be taken from her. Even the most painful memories had a way of helping her face life's challenges.

It had been a bitterly cold day in her hometown in Holland when she had learned there are some things worse than death. Angela's parents both died from pneumonia when she was ten. It was left to her older sister, Eva, to keep house for the two of them. But then, when Angela was thirteen, Eva was taken from her.

Historians labeled that time in history the Holocaust. For Angela, that word didn't do justice to the horrors she had witnessed. Even now, some fifty years later, memories were crystal clear. She and her best friend, Anna, had watched in terror as soldiers came to her home, stole all of her family's material possessions, and then took away the one thing that Angela valued most: her sister.

What sustained Angela through the anguish of the days, weeks, and months that followed were her sister's last words. "Don't be afraid, Angela," Eva had called to her. "No matter what they do to our bodies, they can't injure our faith or the love we have for each other. Look up and remember me when you see the clouds." It was these words, and Eva's great courage as the soldiers shoved her out the door and out of Angela's life, that even now strengthened Angela's resolve to face anything—anywhere—anytime—with faith, not fear.

Angela's thoughts turned to her friend Anna. After Eva's abduction Angela had moved in with Anna's family. The two girls became like sisters; they even immigrated to America together once they were old enough to be on their own. But as close as they were, the suffering they had both witnessed nourished two different types of hearts in them. Angela grew in solid faith, while Anna grew more and more bitter with the years, blaming God for everything that hurt her. Angela felt great compassion for her friend, knowing that God wasn't Anna's enemy; he was her defender, her healer, and her greatest ally when things got tough. If only Anna would believe it!

Now, as Angela sat looking out the hospital window, focusing on the cloud formations, Anna charged into the room. "Have you heard yet?" she demanded. "Have you gotten the results?"

"Anna, sit down," Angela said, patting the side of her bed. "I don't know anything yet. I'm still waiting on the doctor." Angela took her friend's hand and squeezed it.

"How can you be so calm?" Anna cried. "What if the doctor gives you bad news?"

"We have been in tough spots before, you and I," Angela replied. "We are survivors. No matter what the doctor tells me, it only affects my body. It will never change my faith or the love we have for each other."

Anna's eyes turned wistful. She had heard similar words once before. "That's what Eva said," she whispered.

"Yes. And it's true. Nothing that happened on that day destroyed my faith or my love for Eva."

Angela looked up at the clouds, and Anna followed her gaze. "When I look at the sky and see the clouds changing and moving," Angela said, "I remember that Eva wanted me to move and change too. She didn't want me to get stuck in bitterness or hate. She wanted me to use the challenges in life—the things that blow me this way and that—to continually reshape me into a better person."

Angela looked deep into her friend's eyes. "That's what I want for you, Anna. Don't let resentment and anger over things in the past—things that you couldn't control—suffocate you any longer. Move on, like a cloud does with the wind, and don't be afraid of change. Behind every challenge is an opportunity to grow in faith if we will only believe it."

Just as Angela finished her sentence, a knock came on the door, and a doctor stepped into the room. Angela smiled at the serious-looking professional who was probably twenty years her junior. Then she looked at Anna, whose expression seemed calmer and more peaceful than it had been in years. Angela took her friend's hand again and squeezed it. The two old friends were about to be presented with a new challenge, and they would face it together. But this time, perhaps, both would respond with strength and faith, not fear.

EVERY PAINFUL EVENT
CONTAINS IN ITSELF A SEED
OF GROWTH AND LIBREATION.

Anthony de Mello

The LORD is my STRENGTH and my *shield;* my heart *trusts* in *him,* and I am HELPED.

Psalm 28:7

Gentle Strength

Enthusiasm

Touch

Well Wishes

Endless Hope

Laughter

Love

CHAPTER 2

Enthusiasm

The sun is an amazing energy source—an explosion of energy that provides warmth and light to the earth. Clouds may cover it for a time, but its rays always break through to brighten the world once again. Light always dispels the darkness!

Illness, like those clouds, does not have to darken our lives for long. If we are excited about life—if we want to live life to the fullest—our enthusiasm and joy can be an energy source that speeds us on toward wellness. It can ignite a fire of strength and resolve that no manner of sickness can extinguish.

Go ahead—explode with enthusiasm. You have so much ahead of you! Shine brightly as you improve day by day.

GET WELL!

APATHY CAN ONLY BE OVERCOME
BY ENTHUSIASM, AND ENTHUSIASM
CAN ONLY BE AROUSED
BY TWO THINGS: FIRST, AN IDEAL
WHICH TAKES THE IMAGINATION BY
STORM, AND SECOND,
A DEFINITE PLAN FOR CARRYING
THAT IDEAL INTO PRACTICE.

Arnold Toynbee

THERE ARE TWO WAYS
TO LIVE YOUR LIFE.
ONE IS AS THOUGH
NOTHING IS A MIRACLE.
THE OTHER IS AS THOUGH
EVERYTHING IS A MIRACLE.

Albert Einstein

• Motivated Persistence •

At no time in the last fifteen years had Carol seen such a badly injured patient come into her rehab clinic for physical therapy. Brad had been crushed in a car accident, and most of the bones below his neck had been broken, some shattered more than others. He was in a coma for three days after the accident. He was not expected to live, much less regain consciousness. When the doctors realized that he'd willed himself to survive, the prognosis they delivered to the family was not bright, but he'd beaten those odds too.

This man who was told he would never sit up was now able to take five steps before he had to rely on the walker his children had decorated with snapshots of earlier days. Brad had a goal, and he was bound and determined to reach it.

Three times a week, Brad visited the rehab clinic, always arriving sharply at 9:45 in the morning. He had scheduled his visits so that he could deliver his children to school in the specially equipped van that would accommodate his wheelchair, his walker, and his children. He would drop them off and then head for the clinic to begin his grueling schedule of exercises.

The first thing that impressed Carol about Brad was the fact that whenever he was spoken to, he always responded with a smile. He accepted help when he needed guidance for improving performance on the equipment he used. He accepted direction to increase the physical demands on his body without ever once complaining about the pain or whining that he just couldn't take any more. Carol began to wonder if he knew the words *I can't*. He never seemed daunted by the length of time it took him to show improvement.

Brad never failed to leave the facility without telling someone to have a great day. He took every opportunity to encourage the other patients—especially the older ones. He knew their children and grandchildren and inquired about their lives. He listened with a sympathetic ear and gave warm hugs when appropriate. He also took the time to know the staff at the clinic. Brad was an encouragement to everyone he came in contact with.

Carol watched and worked with Brad for more than a year before she approached him about his gift of encouragement.

"Brad, you've come a long way in the last year," she said. "You never seem discouraged when the process is slow, and you don't complain when the pain seems intense. I know you are in pain because I see it on your face. What can you share with me that I can pass on to my other patients?"

Brad sat silently, apparently puzzled at the thought that someone had been watching him. After a moment he pointed to the snapshots embellishing his walker.

"The faces in those pictures are my motivation," he said. "After the accident I realized that I had been given a second chance to reassess the priorities in my life. I have to walk for my children. Even if I never walk more than five steps, I have to teach by my example how to face adversity. I could sit and let bitterness and anger consume me and ruin the lives of my family, or I can show them that I am more than just the broken body they see each day. I am determined to show them that no matter what life hands them, they can face it."

Brad's enthusiastic determination left Carol speechless.

"Why do you take the time to speak to the other patients when you could spend that energy on your recovery?"

"I believe that the encouragement we share with each other is a big part of the therapy here. The success of one in therapy is shared by us all and sends the message that we all need to keep trying."

As Brad returned to his leg-strengthening exercises, Carol stopped to survey his progress for a moment. As she watched, he turned to say something to the older man on the treadmill beside him. Carol believed that Brad's persistence may very well enable him to walk, but his heart would always be stronger than his legs.

THE GREATER PART
OF OUR HAPPINESS OR MISERY
DEPENDS ON OUR DISPOSITIONS, AND
NOT ON OUR CIRCUMSTANCES.

Martha Washington

THEY shall obtain *gladness* and *joy;* and *sorrow* and MOURNING shall *flee* away.

Isaiah 51:11 KJV

Gentle Strength

Enthusiasm

Touch

Well Wishes

Endless Hope

Laughter

Love

CHAPTER 3

Touch

Getting well takes every bit of resolve we can muster, both emotionally and physically. What sustains us and strengthens us in this process? The gentle encouragement of a close friend. A touch of love from a family member. A pat on the hand from a caring nurse. A doctor's kindly message of hope. Those who care for us and care about us nudge us on with their gentle touches.

I want to stand hand in hand with you right now and say, "You will get better. The days ahead are brighter." Consider yourself touched!

GET WELL!

To array a man's will
against his sickness
is the supreme art of medicine.

Henry Ward Beecher

I will *heal* my people
and will let them *enjoy*
ABUNDANT peace
and *security*.

Jeremiah 33:6

MORE THAN MACHINERY,
WE NEED HUMANITY.
MORE THAN CLEVERNESS,
WE NEED KINDNESS AND
GENTLENESS. WITHOUT THESE
QUALITIES, LIFE WILL BE VIOLENT,
AND ALL WILL BE LOST.

Charlie Chaplin

• The Game Plan •

This battle had been fought for years, but the two warriors took their places across the table from each other again. On one side sat the self-assured, mighty man of medicine, the doctor. On the other sat the strong-willed, battle-weary opponent, the mother. Both were ready to discuss and dissect the plan that was to be presented. Both carried equal weight when it came to making a decision about the plan, and the other knew it.

The subject of discussion was fifteen-year-old Taylor who suffered with chronic fatigue. The symptoms had not shown themselves for the last year, but had now returned. The discussion today concerned a new treatment for the syndrome. The new plan of action included daily physical therapy, which may be all that Taylor would have the strength to accomplish in a given day, and dietary counseling that would involve a new set of doctors. Both new types of treatment would put greater demands on the entire family, as well as bring changes in their style and routine of daily living.

"Why are the symptoms returning?" was the first question fired across the table.

"I don't have a definite answer for that one," the answer shot back.

"Why this new plan of therapy?" the question rapidly followed.

"Because this is one treatment we haven't tried yet, and in researching this case, I found studies show that this treatment may bring about an improvement," came the reply.

Questions and answers about the suggested course of action quickly bounced back and forth across the table until both were physically and emotionally spent. The agony of decision was dreadful, but finally the resolution agreed upon was to proceed.

A concerned silence hung in the air. The doctor leaned across the table and gently touched the hand of the mother. Both knew the emotional climate in the room would soon change.

The doctor opened the door.

Taylor shuffled in, physically drained, dreading the next few minutes when he would hear what his body was to undergo next. He sat down in the vacant chair and braced himself to hear what the next round of treatment would require of him.

"Come on in, Taylor," Dr. Mike said. Long ago the formality of last names had been dropped.

Dr. Mike sat down on the stool and turned to face Taylor.

"Sit down, Kathy, while Taylor and I talk."

The doctor took a deep breath and put his hand on Taylor's shoulder.

"I am so sorry that the fatigue has returned. I wish I could give you a pill and tell you that you would feel better in three days. I can't do that. But I do have something new we can try that I think will make a difference."

Dr. Mike spent the next few minutes explaining in as much detail as possible what Taylor could expect with the treatment over the next few weeks. Kathy sat silently and watched Taylor's face as he listened to the doctor. Relief swept over her as she saw Taylor accept the new direction they would travel, but the greatest relief came as she saw the look that told her he was listening to a friend.

"Do you have any questions, Taylor?" the doctor asked.

"When do we start?"

This question signaled that there would be no resistance.

Dr. Mike put his arm around Taylor and hugged him in

a way that he knew a fifteen-year-old boy would accept.

"Taylor, I wish I could tell you that I could make your problems go away and never return. I will tell you that I know your condition has given you chronic heart pain because you feel guilty about the time your family spends dealing with it and that it hurts because of the way it affects your life. You have to miss out on so much. I have watched you grow up with this burden. I have prayed for relief for you, and I have prayed a prayer of thankfulness for the strength and dignity you have shown. I have to tell you that you have taught me that sometimes a hug and a listening ear are the best medicine I can give. I can promise you that I will be here when you need to talk or when you need not to talk. I will be here when you need to cry because you're frustrated or scream at somebody because you are angry. Promise me that you will call when you need me."

Taylor looked up at his friend. "I promise," he said with a grin, and shuffled out of the room.

The two adults faced each other again knowing that now they were facing the battle from the same side. They were now carrying the same banner—a banner that Taylor was too weak to carry for himself.

Let *your*
gentleness
be EVIDENT
to *all.*

Philippians 4:5

Gentle Strength

Enthusiasm

Touch

Well Wishes

Endless Hope

Laughter

Love

CHAPTER 4

Well Wishes

Wishes for a speedy recovery can convey a range of emotions. One wish might express a cheerful greeting, another an urgent plea. However they're expressed, get-well wishes always convey messages of love, compassion, and concern. When illness gets us down, these wishes pick us back up again. Knowing that someone else cares and wants the best for us encourages us and helps lift the burden in the struggle to get well. We are not fighting alone.

My wish for you is that you be well in body and in spirit. Get well soon!

GET WELL!

Just as there comes a warm sunbeam into every cottage window, so comes a love-beam of God's care and pity for every separate need.

Nathaniel Hawthorne

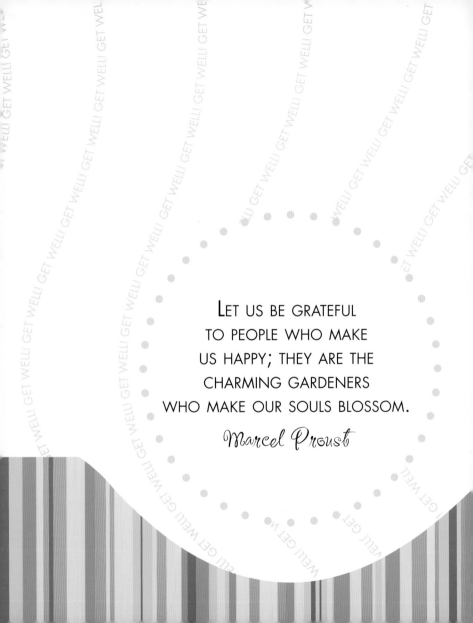

LET US BE GRATEFUL
TO PEOPLE WHO MAKE
US HAPPY; THEY ARE THE
CHARMING GARDENERS
WHO MAKE OUR SOULS BLOSSOM.

Marcel Proust

• Stars of Happiness •

The nursing staff changed every night at 7:00 p.m., and for the last five nights, Rosa had found herself in charge of the grumpy old man in Room 3450: Mr. Ben McAllister.

Mr. McAllister was recuperating from major heart surgery. The doctors said his prognosis was good if his spirits could just be lifted. It was amazing, but Rosa saw it time and time again: people who drew strength from the support and encouragement of others, who felt they had a reason to live, improved much more quickly than those who pushed others away and remained pessimistic about life.

A handful of friends and family members had come to visit Mr. McAllister earlier in the week, but Rosa noticed that he always dismissed them rather quickly. He was in a great deal of pain, and sometimes it seemed to Rosa that he just wanted to stay that way.

But tonight Rosa had come to work with a plan. She was going to deliver a special message to Mr. Ben McAllister.

She swept into his room with a cheerful smile. "Hello,

Mr. McAllister," she said as she reached for his wrist to check his vital signs. "I have a surprise for you. Some children from my church make cards for me to give to my patients. I saved a very special one for you."

Rosa placed the card on the table beside the bed.

"Thanks, but no thanks," growled her patient. "You can take it to someone who needs it."

Rosa ignored his gruffness. "After you read it, I'll tell you about the little girl who made it," she responded lightly, checking his IV. "I'll be back in about an hour."

As Rosa left the room, Ben McAllister settled back on his pillows with a sigh of resignation. He stared out the window blankly until the sun was finally gone and the darkness of the night filled the room. He sat in the darkness for several minutes before reaching for the button to turn on the bedside light.

In the soft glow of the single light bulb, he noticed the card Rosa had left on the table. Frowning, he picked it up and read the message at the top:

"Sometimes when things look dark, you have to look hard to find a way to be happy. Hold this card up to the light. I hope it will make you smile."

When Ben opened the card, he found that the inside

was dark, like the night sky. Curious, he held the card up to the bedside lamp and saw that someone had taken a star-shaped hole puncher and used it to make a random design around the edge of the card. In the middle of the card, the holes formed a happy face.

As hard as he tried, Ben could not keep the corners of his mouth from turning up a bit. He turned the card over and found the rest of the message:

"If you look up to see what has been created for you, then you have to realize the world is filled with love and happiness."

At the bottom of the card was a note written in cursive, with a flower drawn to dot the *i* in the signer's name:

"I hope you get well soon and go back to the ones who love you. Nita."

Ben put the card back on the table, leaving it open so the light came through and he could still see the design. He didn't notice as Rosa peeked into the room, smiled, and pushed open the door.

"Mr. McAllister," she said, "there is someone I want you to meet, if you don't mind."

"You're not going to let me say no, are you?" Ben asked.

Rosa chuckled. "I'd like you to meet the child who made

the card. But, if you refuse, I won't make you do it," she said.

"Oh, all right. Come on in, and bring your friend," Ben answered, trying not to sound too interested.

Rosa left the room and returned a moment later, holding the hand of a small, frail child. The child was completely bald, so it took Ben a few seconds to realize that his visitor was a little girl about ten years old.

"Mr. McAllister, this is Nita. She is just finishing up some tests after her last round of chemo. She wanted to meet the person who received her card."

Ben was a bit tongue-tied as he looked at the little girl standing before him and remembered the words of hope and strength she had written in her card.

"Thank you for the card," he finally said over the lump that had risen in his throat. "It was very pretty. I know it took a lot of time to put the holes in just the right places."

"Oh, I love to make cards," Nita said softly. "I can't play or go to school, so I spend a lot of time making cards for people in the hospital. My mom and my nurses keep bringing me paper and pens. I love getting cards, so I figure others do too. Everybody needs to know that someone cares about them."

To his surprise, Ben found himself fighting back tears.

"Have you been sick long?" Nita asked.

"I've been sick for a couple of months, but I think now that the surgery is over, I will feel much better," Ben answered, suddenly realizing that his pain had subsided sometime that evening.

"Well, I had better go," Nita said. "My parents are tired, and they're waiting for me back in my room so they can say good-bye before they go home. It's very hard on them, you know, watching me go through all these tests."

Nita waved as she turned to leave. "I really do hope you get well soon," she said.

"I hope the results from your tests are good," Ben responded. "And Nita, I want you to know that your card was just what I needed. Every time I look at it, I will think of you."

Nita replied with a bright smile and left the room holding Rosa's hand.

"Thank you, Nita," Ben called out, feeling stronger than he had in weeks. He hesitated a moment. "And thank you, Rosa," he added.

Rosa was already down the hall, but not too far to hear those last words. She squeezed Nita's hand and smiled.

GET WELL!

GOD CANNOT GIVE US A HAPPINESS AND PEACE APART FROM HIMSELF, BECAUSE IT IS NOT THERE. THERE IS NO SUCH THING.

C. S. Lewis

Beloved,
I *pray* that *you*
may *prosper* in
all *things* and be in
health, just as your
soul *prospers*.

3 John 2 NKJV

Gentle Strength

Enthusiasm

Touch

Well Wishes

Endless Hope

Laughter

Love

CHAPTER 5

Endless Hope

The belief that there is always another road to be traveled is what leads to the highway called hope. This highway has no dead ends—only new beginnings. Only by traveling this road will we find what is truly good in life. Only by traveling this road will we learn the new lessons that are just waiting to be learned.

When we're ill, our need for hope is especially great. But if we just look beyond the next turn, if we keep the future as our destination, we will find the strength and the will to stay the course.

Here's hoping for brighter days and safe travel as you continue down the road to good health!

GET WELL!

HOPE IS NOT THE CONVICTION THAT
SOMETHING WILL TURN OUT WELL
BUT THE CERTAINTY THAT
SOMETHING MAKES SENSE,
REGARDLESS OF HOW IT TURNS OUT.

Vaclav Havel

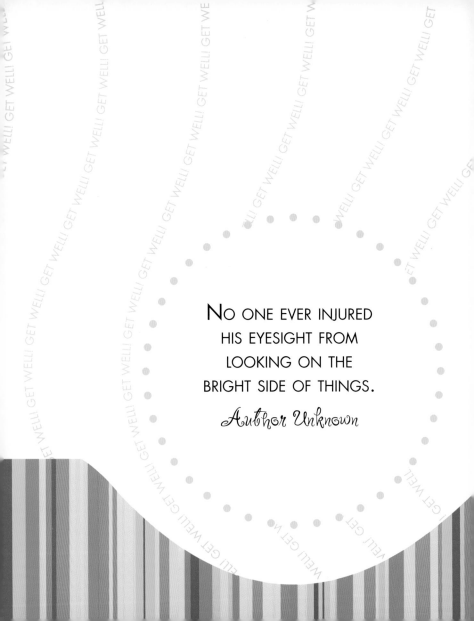

No one ever injured
his eyesight from
looking on the
bright side of things.

Author Unknown

• The Greatest Gift •

Mary Williams's family congregated in her hospital room to hear t he cardiologist's report. Her only hope, the doctor told them in a grave but kindly voice, was open-heart surgery. Yes, the surgery involved risks, and he explained them in detail. But not having the surgery was risky as well. When he finished, he left the room so that Mary and her grown children could talk about their options.

Mary was nearly eighty years old and had long ago learned to accept life as it came to her. After listening to her children's opinions, she sent them out of the room so she could spend some quiet time in prayer. She knew this was not the kind of decision that should rest with one of her children; there were too many things that could go wrong. She didn't want them to squabble or feel guilty later if the surgery didn't have the desired results.

She prayed until she felt at peace with her decision and then called her family back into the room. She smiled as she watched each of them enter and take their places around the room, obviously anxious for her answer. Her oldest son, Alex, stood near the door and tapped his toe. She knew that she could trust him to carry out her wishes. Next to the bedside table was Dale, who possessed the tender heart of his late father. His eyes appeared moist, and he looked down at the floor. The youngest, Jennifer, took a seat at the foot of the bed and held her mother's hand. Jennifer would grieve the most if something went wrong, Mary knew, but she would also stand firmest in her faith that God was in control, no matter what. She was a lot like her mother.

"Now listen," Mary said matter-of-factly. "Let's deal with reality. I want to live, so I am going to have the doctors do this procedure as soon as possible. I have talked to God about it, and I have a great deal of hope that everything will go well."

Her voice took on a firmer tone. "But in case something happens, there are some things that we need to settle now," she continued. "I have made a list of my possessions that I would like to pass down to you. Each of you has told me of one thing that carries sentimental value for you, and I have honored your requests. I have also divided up a number of other things in a way that I think is fair and equitable. Everything else is to be divided equally among the grandchildren. I want them to have something that reminds them of their feisty old grandmother."

"But, Mother—," Jennifer objected.

"Hush, now, and let me finish," Mary said, patting Jennifer's hand. "Then you can have your say. In my top dresser drawer you will find a list of the songs I want sung at my funeral, as well as a list of the people I want to help conduct it. I have chosen my favorite songs, and they're not ones that are usually sung at a funeral. I didn't include any of those sad, wailing songs. None of us likes to hear them now, and I don't want you to have to suffer through them after I'm dead!"

The siblings glanced at one another, exchanging nervous smiles.

"I want my funeral to be a celebration of the life I have lived," Mary said. "Have the preacher tell about the time I chased the squatters off my father's farm with a shotgun at the age of twelve. Have him tell about how your father and I met working in the fields to make money to buy school clothes. And don't let him forget the day I ran over the cow with the tractor.

"Most importantly, make sure that someone tells about the faith that your father and I have passed on to you children. I want people to know about the hope that has always enabled our family to keep going, even through the tough times."

Noticing the tears welling up in her children's eyes, Mary added with a twinkle, "And whatever you do, don't bury me in a navy blue dress. Navy blue takes the color right out of my cheeks!"

"Only you, Mother, would worry about that," Dale said, smiling with his brother and sister.

At that moment the doctor gave a quick rap on the door and entered the room.

"Have you made a decision?" he asked.

Mary looked him squarely in the eyes. "Schedule the operation as soon as possible," she announced. "I want to be home before the bulbs start blooming in my front yard."

The doctor nodded his head and turned to go. Alex shook the doctor's hand as he left the room.

When Mary spoke again, her voice was softer.

"I want to live a full life in the time I have left on this earth," she said, looking first at Alex, then Dale, then Jennifer. "I believe this operation will enable me to do so. I don't want to die, but I'm not afraid to go. Either way, I have a hope and a confidence that gives me peace. I know that no matter what the outcome of the surgery is, I will awaken to a celebration."

Alex stepped up to the bed and kissed his mother gently on the cheek. "I've got to get back to work now, Mother," he said. "I'll see you first thing tomorrow."

Dale kissed his mother too. "Sarah and the kids are waiting for me in the lobby," he said. "They send their love. I'll bring the twins up to see you tomorrow."

Next, Jennifer moved up from her place at the foot of the bed, kissed her mother's cheek, and threw her arms around her neck. Neither she nor her mother moved for several minutes.

Finally, Jennifer released her hold and began to make her way to the door.

"Where are you going?" Mary asked.

"I'm going to go mulch the bulbs in your yard, Mother, so they'll be ready for your homecoming," Jennifer replied with a smile, closing the door behind her.

Now *faith* is
being *sure* of what
we *hope* for
and CERTAIN of what
we *do not see.*

Hebrews 11:1

GET WELL!

HOPE IS WISHING FOR
A THING TO COME TRUE;
FAITH IS BELIEVING
THAT IT WILL COME TRUE.

Norman Vincent Peale

Gentle Strength

Enthusiasm

Touch

Well Wishes

Endless Hope

Laughter

Love

CHAPTER 6

Laughter

The world's most celebrated wise man once said, "A merry heart doeth good like a medicine" (Proverbs 17:22 KJV). But in this day of new and improved drugs designed to cure anything that ails you, the medicine of laughter is often overlooked. The fact is, a good belly laugh expends calories and changes the brain's chemical balance. The benefits of laughter are scientifically proven! Instead of moping around the house, reflecting on the crisis at hand, we need to give ourselves permission to laugh—a lot. It will bring great peace and put us on the road to better health.

Go ahead. Have a good laugh! It will do you good.

GET WELL!

He who laughs, LASTS.

Mary Pettibone Poole

• Laughing Song •

When the green woods laugh with the voice of joy,
And the dimpling stream runs laughing by;
When the air does laugh with our merry wit,
And the green hill laughs with the noise of it;

When the meadows laugh with lively green,
And the grasshopper laughs in the merry scene,
When Mary and Susan and Emily
With their sweet round mouths sing "Ha, ha, he!"

When the painted birds laugh in the shade,

Where our table with cherries and nuts is spread:

Come live, and be merry, and join with me,

To sing the sweet chorus of "Ha, ha, he!"

William Blake

The excursion is the same when you go looking for your sorrow as when you go looking for your joy.

Eudora Welty

GET WELL!

AGAINST THE ASSAULT OF LAUGHTER
NOTHING CAN STAND.

Mark Twain

He will yet *fill*
your *mouth* with
LAUGHTER
and your *lips* with
shouts of JOY.

Job 8:21

Gentle Strength

Enthusiasm

Touch

Well Wishes

Endless Hope

Laughter

Love

CHAPTER 7

Love

To see pure love, we only have to look at a puppy as he ecstatically greets his master. Shaking with anticipation, he leaps into his master's waiting arms and licks his face with unbridled enthusiasm.

We also see pure love when friends, family, and caregivers come bearing wishes for our good health. Their sincere concern washes over us like a healing balm, motivating us to get well.

But we see the purest love of all in the One who promises, "But for you who revere my name, the sun of righteousness will rise with healing in its wings. And you will go out and leap like calves released from the stall" (Malachi 4:2)—or like a puppy into his master's arms.

Go ahead. Leap into his perfect love!

GET WELL!

LOVE WING'D MY HOPES
AND TAUGHT ME HOW TO FLY.

Author Unknown

WHAT THE HEART HAS
ONCE OWNED AND HAD,
IT SHALL NEVER LOSE.

Henry Ward Beecher

• Love Rediscovered •

The *blip-blip-blip* of the heart monitor echoed through Jan's mind as she tried to clear her thoughts. *What do I do next?* she asked herself.

She knew the answer before she finished asking the question: she needed to call Doug, her older brother. But that was not the answer she was hoping for.

The last time she and Doug had been together, they had parted in anger. Since that time their conversations over the phone had been short and to the point. Doug no longer ended with "Luv ya, Peanut," and Jan no longer responded, "Luv ya back, Big Bro"—words of endearment they had exchanged for years. Jan knew that Doug still loved her, and she still loved him. But they had disagreed as they never had before—ever—over whether or not to place Dad in a retirement home. Now their relationship was uncomfortable and their conversations strained.

The sound of her father's heart monitor refocused her thoughts. As long as the *blip-blip-blip* remained steady, did she need to call? Maybe everything would turn out all right and she and Dad would be on their way home soon. Maybe it wasn't a heart attack after all.

No, Jan told herself, *if the roles were reversed, I would want Doug to call me, even if he knew things were OK.* She looked down at her father and saw that he was dozing. Quietly she exited the emergency room and made her way down the hall toward the telephone in the waiting area.

The phone call consisted of three emotion-filled sentences:

"Doug, I'm in the emergency room with Dad. He may have had a heart attack."

"I'm on my way."

The next twenty minutes seemed to crawl by as Jan waited for news—any news—from the doctor. She tried to read a magazine from the stack in the waiting room but found herself looking up toward the doorway every few minutes. It was hard for her to admit it, but she was as anxious to see Doug's face as she was to see the doctor's.

Jan picked up a card that had been left on the table next to the magazines. "Get Well Wishes" it read on the front, just above a colorful picture of a spring bouquet. *Yes, get well wishes to you, Dad,* she thought. Then the wish changed to a silent, urgent plea: *Get well, Dad. Please get well.* Finally the plea became a heartfelt prayer: *Father, help him get well.*

As Jan finished mouthing the words, she heard her name being called. "Miss Walker, the doctor wants to talk to you," a nurse announced. At the same time a familiar voice came from across the room. "Jan," her brother said as he swept through the swinging doors.

Jan felt a rush of relief knowing that she wouldn't have to face the doctor's news alone. "This is my brother, Doug," she said to the nurse. Doug gripped her hand, and they walked down the cold corridor together.

The nurse led them into their father's cubicle. He was awake, and he reached for Jan's free hand.

"Your father had a heart attack," the doctor confirmed from the foot of the bed, "but it was a mild one, and there has been no permanent damage. We're going to keep him in the hospital for a few days, but don't worry. We expect a full recovery."

Jan felt her entire body relax. She felt Doug relax, too, through the lighter clutch of his hand.

Neither one let go.

At that moment Jan realized that she wasn't angry anymore, and neither was Doug. The anger they'd harbored dissipated in the wake of something more important: the common love they felt for their father—and for each other. The issue of the retirement home would have to be faced, but they would leave it for another day. This was a time to embrace life and be thankful for answered prayer. It was a time to appreciate the strength and comfort that comes from the presence of those you love.

"Get well quickly, Dad," Jan said. She leaned over, kissed her father, and then headed back to the waiting room, while Doug lingered to ask the doctor a few more questions. Smiling broadly, she felt as if she were floating down the hall. Everyone who passed her knew in an instant that whatever had happened to her loved one, the prognosis was good.

Little did they know she'd seen more than one kind of trauma treated and healed in the emergency room that day.

Thy love is such I can no way repay,

The heavens reward thee manifold, I pray.

Then while we live,

in love let's so persever,

That when we live no more,

we may live ever.

Anne Bradstreet

There is
no FEAR in love.
But *perfect* LOVE
drives out fear.

1 John 4:18

Get Well!